Dilemmas

Dedication

For Mei-Yee

Dilemmas

William L. Ramsey

Copyright 2015 by Clemson University
ISBN 978-0-9908958-4-8

Published by Clemson University Press in Clemson, South Carolina

Editorial Assistants: Karen Stewart and Charis Chapman

To order copies, please visit the Clemson University Press website: www.clemson.edu/press

Contents

Acknowledgments • viii

❦

First Set: Excluded Middles

A Daguerreotype of Tea Leaves • 2
Encountering the Capitalist Muse • 3
Cleaning the Mermaid • 4
In Medias Res (the Poem) • 5
What the World Is • 6
Tarot Divination • 7
Grievous Angel on State Road 178 • 8
Versions of Brahms • 9
New Orleans Rain • 10
Alice After Katrina • 11
Now What, Genius? • 12
In *My* Medieval Tapestry • 13
Trees, Forest, etc. • 14
Space and Air • 15
Upland Fork • 16
Why I'm So Late • 17
To Be Filed in the Category of Inauspicious Omens • 18
Learning Curve • 19
Navigating New Orleans • 21
The Visit • 22
Origins of Echoes • 23
Call's Creek Loop • 24

Second Set: The Euthyphro Dilemma

To Build Your Own Parthenon • 26
Causal Sequence • 28
Fog's Nest • 29
Sumer is Icumen In • 30

Green Thumb • 31
Liturgical Chant • 32
Dozing with Coffee • 33
Monsieur Transitif • 34
Memorabilia • 35
On Zhao Meng-Fu's "Wang River Scroll" • 36
Name Dropping • 37
The Death of Gérard de Nerval • 38
References • 39
The Phoenix Riot, 1898 • 40
Sydney Lanier Passing Through Asheville, NC, 1881 • 41
The Coelacanth • 42
How It Happened • 43
Southern Crescent • 44
Frog in Ivy • 45
Catullus in the Afterlife • 46
By the Comet's Light • 47
Formalities • 48

Third Set: The Hedgehog's Dilemma

Dialectic • 50
Tryst in Three Dimensions • 51
Elle Fait Une Promenade • 54
Her Laughter • 55
December to June • 56
The Vesuvius of Orreries • 57
Meandering in New Orleans • 58
He Catches Hell • 59
Still-life After a Long Night • 60
The Stressed Syllable • 61
By Lake Pontchartrain • 62
Seven P.M. or So • 63
Parting, with a Sequel • 64
Parking in Bayou Des Égarés • 65
Peasant Wedding Aftermath • 66
An Evening Out with Pharaoh • 67
Islamorada • 68
Running Late in Yuyao • 69

Rhetorical Occasions • 70
A Note on Surplus Value • 72
Ozymandias at Odds • 73
Last Meeting • 74

Acknowledgments

Beloit Poetry Journal: "Running Late in Yuyao"
Buddhist Poetry Review: "On Zhao Meng-Fu's 'Wang River Scroll'" and "Origins of Echoes"
The Externalist: "By Lake Pontchartrain" and "New Orleans Rain"
Hampden-Sydney Poetry Review: "A Daguerreotype of Tea Leaves," "Ozymandias at Odds" and "Sumer Is Icumen In"
Hellas: "The Death of Gerard de Nerval" and "Monsieur Transitif"
Iodine Poetry Journal: "Islamorada" and "Dialectic"
Louisiana Literature: "Elle Fait Une Promenade" and "Meandering in New Orleans"
Lullwater Review: "Encountering the Capitalist Muse"
Mainstreet Rag: "Versions of Brahms"
Mind in Motion: "The Coelacanth"
Old Red Kimono: "Still-Life After a Long Night"
Onionhead: "Tarot Divination"
Plainsongs: "An Evening Out with Pharaoh"
Poetry: "He Catches Hell"
Poetry Northwest: "In Medias Res (the Poem)"
Riverrun: "Dozing with Coffee"
Snake Nation Review: "In My Medieval Tapestry"
The South Carolina Review: "A Note on Surplus Value" and "The Phoenix Riot, 1898"
Southern Poetry Review: "Cleaning the Mermaid" and "The Visit"
Tar River Poetry: "Grievous Angel on State Road 178" and "Formalities"
Town Creek Poetry: "Why I'm So Late"

First Set: Excluded Middles

—Georg Wilhelm Friedrich Hegel, *The Phenomenology of Spirit*: "The bud disappears as the blossom bursts forth, and one could say that the former is refuted by the latter. . . . Their fluid nature, however, makes them, at the same time, elements of an organic unity in which they not only do not conflict, but in which one is as necessary as the other; and it is only this equal necessity that constitutes the life of the whole."

A Daguerreotype of Tea Leaves

One of Chopin's nocturnes, number nine or up,
    thirty-two especially, not heard, not at all, but
    visible in the cratered tin of the tea, the tilted cup.

Or most of Beethoven's sonatas, only it cannot
    be number nine. One may infer this music
    mainly from the tea and the cup and the knot

of brownish haze beyond the wooden bench, keys
    that have bled out into the faded bronze of the sky,
    sheet music blurred into the gut of the breeze,

sepia clouds, coal veins vibrating in the Channel.
    You are alone. Is that not news? But a lover now
    approaches. A floral dress pattern, perhaps flannel,

early 1860s, grayish-tan, articulated by the outline
    of a flexed knee, a gray made slightly lavender
    by the leeching rhythm of mercury, residual brine

of silver nitrate. Or else the lover is already present
    but has not been recognized. Present all along.
    Soon to become known, discernible as mere intent

that narrows in elaboration from a vanishing point
    between the trellis and the sea, smears southward
    in arthritic arcs across the dark horizon's joint.

If not a lover, a helpmate, kindred laborer. None
    will say enemy. But enemy. What is coming is,
    at any rate, the work of many hands, each one

responsible for playing one disaggregated splinter
    from the frayed pianoforte, barely visible above
    Orion before sunrise every fall and early winter.

Encountering the Capitalist Muse

At first, you mistake
her for an advertisement,
her long, blond hair tossed
wildly by an unfelt wind.
You look for the product

hovering in pastel holiness
above her shoulder, but,
finding only some ramshackle
buildings and busted rubbish,
eventually come to sense,

and, as she draws near,
observe how the wind, as
it troubles her hair, sounds
like a sluggish Gershwin song,
how her spinning eyes

like hubcaps turn both
ways at once. You learn
from her kisses to want those
words which carry the water
of chaos like blood-colored

wine in a breath of copper,
and believe in the power
of voices to sell what is
neither here nor there, nor
anything worth ever having.

Cleaning the Mermaid

What to say of it, the fish part,
       that does not sound like
       any fish: rough to the fingers,
       difficult to scale, knife catching on hide,
       platelets glancing off my glasses?

For it is hard enough anyway
       to hold it steady in the sink
       without the soft voice in the ear,
       the plaintive singing, the water in its lungs
       echoing the faucet's laughter.

I suppose it was that, and the easy
       reception of my thumb upon
       its throat, that made me wonder
       if there might be something, this time,
       to feel sad about.

IN MEDIAS RES
(THE POEM)

Assumes a previous occurrence to have
recently transpired, which, of course, it has,
and acts accordingly, averting danger,
narrowed to a mindfulness of all that must
ensue, having scant seconds, and a large heart,
plunges through a miscellaneous aftermath
of tilted lampshades and green shutters,
sure of nothing, through brochures that
advertise beach weekends and bikini-clad
young women, but, but, no, it stays here
to see justice done, has a beef with destiny,
and just as things look darkest, just as things . . .

What the World Is

They told us just like
they tell everyone

in open gasping fields
in dim hot waves of sun

leaning sometimes on a hoe
leaning others on a gun

what the world is
what is done.

Beyond the hedge however
beyond the snapdragon

where the creek slows
where the waters run

between boulders wedged
between the bright cold beams of sun

we know whatever the world is
we have done.

Tarot Divination

Where better to begin
than with the girl in
the grape arbor who holds
up a hooded falcon?

Principle figure in a
renaissance landscape,
how would she look
in a regular suburb,

water-sprinklers
instead of olive trees
on either side of her,
a tricycle at her feet?

As she sternly gazes
at the bird of prey
perched on her gloved hand,
would she still

represent "discernment,"
"certitude," in her period
costume, or simply
get a job, the tenuous

cobweb meanings
scattered by her breath
as she tells someone
her name, the bird having

roused from her flustered
hand, thrown off its
hood, and fled to
a rooftop antenna?

Grievous Angel on State Road 178

Not until I am ten miles, maybe twelve,
outside Greenwood city limits do I remember
that Emmylou sings duet with Gram Parsons
on "Hickory Wind," and it is too late.

I have already turned off toward Epworth,
almost even with Simpson's Auto Salvage.
Already, I can hear the 1960s models honking
through the rusted chain-link fence ahead.

I look to see if any footpaths have been
worn to the Thunderbird since last time,
and she enters, more cautiously than I recalled,
unsure, perhaps, about what Parsons wants.

It is a live version. A beer bottle breaks
near the microphone, and the shards of glass
continue chiming as a waitress, I'm guessing,
sweeps them up. Better than drums or bass.

Only now, as if she knows whose drink
it was, does she breathe all her wind in the sails
of the song. Ah, hell . . . nothing but pine trees
and maples from here to Mays Crossing.

Versions of Brahms

Well, I only have so many,
    and in the best of them,
    by the Vienna Philharmonic,
    the same woman coughs in the same place
    every time, overlapping the oboes' lingering
    exit.

And it always startles me
    as I wait for the entry of the violins.

I am the only one apparently.
    For all the fifteen years
    I've listened to this version,
    everyone in the audience that night
    continues staring politely at the stage,
    as they do on the album cover, hoping
    for the best.

But I've had it. I turn in my seat tonight
    to look for her.

There is so little light below
    the balcony, it is hard
    to see her features; her dark brown hair
    hangs partially across her face. But there she is,
    her hand still covering her mouth.

She pretends to concentrate
    on the music, but it is clear enough
    she sees me.

She seems, in fact, to have been waiting
    a very long time for someone
    to turn like this, attempt a silent reproach.
    For without much delay, she sweeps her hair
    back and glares at me defiantly. What an
    asshole.

New Orleans Rain

This is the weather Bienville had in mind:
the Gallic overcast, the soggy desuetude.
Tourists drink in bars while residents lean idly

in doorways and windows, watching the place
dissolve, blur inward with reflected light,
fragments of forgotten jazz. The purpose

of noise, they know, is not the splitting blunder
of the saxophone but the pauses between thunder,
when puddles focus briefly before falling back to slivers.

Alice After Katrina

Smaller? Larger?
    It makes no difference.
    The house bears no relation
    to me any longer. The studs and plaster
    soak up all the errant vapors, the fermented
    exhalations, of my last, concerned
    aside.

Following which, I pick a cricket up
    and never speak again of egress or its opposite.

It rubs its wings together,
    and I feel how water hurts itself
    unendingly within the aqueduct,
    discomfiture broken into multiple lesser
    discomfitures that recombine and break again
    as needed.

Even my bones, already
    splintered beyond certain grasp,
    continue snapping on themselves;
    I reach with only sinew after central aspects
    of the soul's intestine, clutching inward.

Thumbs over thumbs
    fetch deeper and deeper
    for indices, footnotes, dim variants
    of gowned light, chess pieces, that warp away
    as if descending through dark water. Everything
    turns to this one task in the end, arcing always
    into voids through which a point of light
    is falling.

A few billion years later,
    I find myself sitting
    at the kitchen table; I have still
    not lifted my cup, and the sunlight lingers
    where it was above the windowsill, spreading
    a small fan of warmth across my swollen
    fingers.

Now What, Genius?

Who will change the world's bandages
        now that the Black-Faced Honeycreeper
        is extinct? The White-Eyed River Martin?

The Carolina Parakeet? Who will plump
        the world's pillow and pull its pressure
        stockings up to its knees and organize

its pills in compartments labeled M, T, W,
        TH, F, SAT? The Koa Finch? The White-
        Winged Sandpiper? The Slender-Billed

Grackle? The Cozumel Thrasher? Crap,
        why don't we toss in a Pterodactyl while
        we're at it? Oh yeah, and a compartment

with a radiant yellow smiling sun on it.
        Well, it won't be the Black-Faced Honey-
        creeper, baby girl. The Black-Faced Honey-

creeper is done flying down from the Gum
        Myrtle Tree every time the world coughs or
        accidentally rolls over on that stupid button.

In *My* Medieval Tapestry

The people would look
awkward too, fearing
to risk movement in a
lawless foreground of
confused perspectives,
tangled points of view,
uncertain, even, whether
to walk toward the eye-
level spread of fruit or
simply put their hands
out for the purple melons.
They too would stand,
stockstill, feigning a fixed
center of haloed saints
to set their eyes upon,
averse to acknowledge
or condone the disarray
that drenches them, the
sickening tilt and sway
of a fallen world that is
never far enough away

TREES, FOREST, ETC.

Hard to tell from here, with the wind leaning
    on the pine boughs and the light so broken,

who's up there by the fallen Boxelder. There
    are not two friends in twelve, fifty years into it,

who would lift a foot across that log to see me
    on the other side. One of them, if I remember

rightly, is out in Idaho, legs tangled in the legs
    of Plato, rolling and laughing like a hoplite

in winter wheat. Hard to tell from here, with
    shadows broken and the pine boughs leaning

on the wind, who it is up there, resting a foot
    on the Boxelder. I suppose I'll stand here one

more minute, just in case, maybe two. But I'd
    be damned sure who's down here, if I were you.

SPACE AND AIR

Spaces that do not fit with any solid objects,
> nor provide adequate electrical outlets or lighting.
> As if one desired to walk from the sewing room
> at Monticello into the kitchen pantries without
> passing through the central hall. Spaces separated
> from each other by other spaces and long silences
> that end with awkward silences. The way the Sea
> and Air section at the National Museum of Air

and Space overlooks the Gemini VII capsule
> at the bottom of the escalator. And the voice down
> the central hallway from the kitchen changes
> nothing. Spaces filled with memories of cardboard
> boxes filled with Christmas ornaments and obsolete
> receipts and cardboard. Not even the voices
> of James Lovell or Frank Borman from orbit.
> Spaces between letters in misspelled words that

do not fit with other words in serviceable sentences
> and, so, develop no ideas or themes, provide no
> context or supporting evidence. Like that time
> we carried a picnic out to the middle of the Reedy
> River, jumping from stone to stone, waiting on each
> other in turn, extending hands to help, debating
> which stones would work best, and left the soda
> in the trunk. Spaces between strands of hair. Spaces

between strands of hair that hang from separate heads
> and move toward each other rapidly in lust or anger,
> wishing to shape themselves around desired objects
> or destroy the objects they detest. Whether upside
> down above the Indian Ocean or pausing to hear
> a voice from the kitchen. Spaces between tongues
> and fingers stained with the desperation of other
> spaces that do not fit with any solid objects.

UPLAND FORK

Why anyone would come this way, where ferns
confuse the pilgrim with perpetual displays
of furled unfurling, and the sunlight yearns
for shadow from the perch of its own rays,
escapes me. Evidence of their passage stays,
nevertheless, once the final footprint turns
and, losing faith, stumbles back toward the bay's
calm waters: torn clothing, echoes of a lantern's
light still clinging to a sandwich crust. A few
went further, maybe, but left no advice
that would be helpful where the sandy loam
gives way to rock. Don't ask me how or who.
Tellers of such stories, those who tell them twice,
remember less and less the way back home.

Why I'm So Late

A very slow vine was not yet finished
    climbing the last deliberate centimeter up my
    spine,

and the pearl-black flower that finally
    blossomed, withering behind my face before it fully
    unfolded,

made several goldfish circle back, deeper
    than usual, before drifting forever into the bridge's
    shade.

To Be Filed in the Category
of Inauspicious Omens

Something buzzes hip high under my arm
       the instant I open the door. Something

black with blackish fuzz and a blue-black
       panoply of golden spikes, maybe best

understood, I now think, as a type of broken,
       yellow banding, buzzes in from the sun's

glare. So I stand, staring at every shadow in
       the hall, listening, at the ready, but find

nothing less dark than the rest of my house
       nor anything louder than me leaving it.

Learning Curve

As I open the car door,
>   you pause, pulling at my hand.
>   >   There was a butterfly today.

So I kneel to hear about it,
>   knowing how much you love them,
>   >   the colors of their wings,

how they fly, how one
>   of them sat next to you once
>   >   while you drank your apple juice.

But the usual question,
>   what color was it, falls flat. You
>   >   look away at the trees, worried.

Yellow and black, you offer
>   after a while; yellow with lots
>   >   of little black circles and one big

black circle in the center
>   of each wing. Sounds pretty,
>   >   I say, but it only makes you cry.

It landed on the playground,
>   right in front of you, flexed its
>   >   wings up and down, unafraid.

Then your friend saw it too.
>   He ran over, stomped his shoe.
>   >   You pushed and shouted, but he

stomped again and again,
>   thinking it funny, shifting his
>   >   foot back and forth. You show me,

like a grown-up stepping
>   on a cigarette, twisting. When
>   >   he stopped, the butterfly was still.

It had a hole in its wing. It
>   had a hole in its wing. You keep
>   >   telling me, pulling me to fix it.

But, son, we're in such a
        hurry to get home, I say. How
                much can anyone learn in one day?

Navigating New Orleans

Two mornings now, an orange-billed pelican
        has descended into Esplanade Canal, its blue-beige
        neck curled back along its body as I turned on Esplanade
        to proceed upriver toward Clearview.

Yesterday, I saw it coming from a hundred
        yards away, rocking above the trees. Not because
        of wind, its neck already tucked for the descent, its legs
        trailing like a kite-tail, but because

its wings were fighting thermals from warm
        pavement, warm canal water, in a slow gentle sweep.
        So slow, as I passed it, I began to think of other things
        before it disappeared below the bank:

thoughts like the banks of the canal itself,
        littered with light, ambient digressions of powdered
        dimness, disintegration's pomp new-flowered, melted
        into canopies of maple and crepe myrtle.

Today, however, it was already eye level
        as I flicked my turn signal on and waited for traffic
        to clear. I theorized about illicit love as Jerry Lee's piano
        pulled even with me in a line of cars,

and before I could straighten out the wheel
        its wings were dusting the tops of the dandelions,
        disappearing into the canal right next to me. I watched
        in the mirror all the way to Clearview

but saw nothing of its long thin legs reaching
        down from sky to water, water up again to sky, stepping
        through themselves to stand on stillness in the end.
        Tomorrow morning, I will take I-10.

The Visit

Vines, braided in vines, pulled from the door.
Cobwebs more numerous, the nearer you come.
They clutch a tarnished knocker close to the wood
but cringe at a candle, recoil from a breath of rum.

You pause instinctively, let silence soak
between your toes to sod, time and time again,
unsure of what you hear inside. A footfall? A news-
paper tossed on a table? Snatched up? Flung again?

A shadow falling, levering down like a leaf,
the shape of it changing as it tumbles? A strip
of ribbon rather than a leaf! A voice? So much like
a dry, brown leaf you stop and listen after every step?

Even as you take the knocker in your hand
you hear what may be dust motes in a shaft of light:
planetesimals, debris fields, collapsing in a plummet
that returns them all to roughly the same height.

Think hard as you lift it. And yet again wait!
Will you listen one last time before you let it drop?
For, afterward, there is no room for doubt. Whatever
is about to fall, or may be falling, will forever stop.

Origins of Echoes

There is no cleverness that can obscure
        the issue more than a decade. The kernel

of it lasts when the body has begun to waste
        and finally shines out from the mind's foil,

shredding memory with shrill immediacy:
        the dry shell wet with the sound of water.

Call's Creek Loop

Is this, after so many summers,
        the same familiar maple on
        the pinewood path again? The solitary
        mountain laurel, leaning out as always
        into sun? How many

million leaves have fallen since I
        climbed down the rocks here,
        through briars and bear grass, to the quiet
        stream, the flat, meandering clouds, half-
        moons, the birdsong

tangled in the interstice of twig
        and twig? How many petals have
        circled briefly since? My knees moist
        on the mossy stones again, hands cupping
        water's coolness I recall.

SECOND SET: THE EUTHYPHRO DILEMMA

—Plato, *Euthyphro*: "Is the pious loved by the gods because he is pious, or is he pious because he is loved by the gods?"

To Build Your Own Parthenon

You will need one fulcrum
        and a V-groove chisel.

Be careful to review any
        restrictive covenants that may

apply. And a lever. There
        will be some bending down,

bringing the elbows level
        with the knees, some

lifting with the legs. All *that*
        is in the manuals already.

But when Doric fluting
        rises from Ionic bases,

when the triglyphs funnel
        rainwater into standing

troughs along the frieze,
        it takes more than a fulcrum.

For this, you must sit
        on the stairs like a stone

too heavy to lift. Kick
        at some pebbles. Consider

them at rest. Some days
        you'll forget your lunch.

You'll want to go home,
        toss in the trowel, work

with something lighter
        than limestone: more

beautiful, more willing
        to receive a polish. But

wait a year or two, when
        others have gone home,

when the dew has frozen
        on the webs. A stubborn

light will stumble from
        the cypress grove, bending

the cold leaves back against
        cold bark, grasping cypress

knees for balance. It will
        loiter awhile at the foot

of the stairs, smelling of figs
        and grapevines and olives,

dissembling, as if it means
        to visit somewhere else

instead. It may stand there
        so long, in fact, you forget

how it feels to be warm,
        see clearly, until it stubs

its brightness on a step
        and falls across your feet.

Causal Sequence

A monk rings a bell,
    a brown, bronze bell,
        and both his eyelids close,

but only now does
    the startled butterfly
        rise up from a nearby rose.

Fog's Nest

Fog swirls in the wake of a butterfly's
        wings and slowly settles in an empty

bird nest for a while. But it cannot rest
        for long. Two vines braid higher and higher

around the tree trunk. One we shall label
        Leonard Cohen, for it hooks its tendrils

over the craggy edges of the bark
        and pulls itself straight up without concern

for artifice. The other we label
        Cassius Clay, since it refuses to serve

in the armed forces. When the sun comes out,
        the spray of the falls begins with a lurch.

Its distant roaring ricochets like fragments
        of bird shell through the branches. It catches

here and there on twiggy crotches. So Clay
        and Cohen pause to eat their sandwiches,

to plot the path of their final ascent,
        watching the fog hop and flap in the nest.

Sumer Is Icumen In

—a seasonal bukakke

Kneaded swath of beaded pearls,
       which in our necklace strings
       affection, lay on the springtime's
       cricketed neck

in lurid, pearl-white strands;
       roll down the autumn's
       ripe, ingenuous throat
       the way a wave, once broken, rolls
       back down the hull of a boat.

Or laying rather on the winter's
       face the way the moonlight lays

upon the sea, its memory
       broken by the water's
       eyes until it seems a set
       of sunken stars, a shattered sun,
       shine like pearls among a deepness,
       darkness, known by none.

Green Thumb

Being tendered in so vested a conceit
        of nubile barter, so incestuous, so spackled

with nuptial twinges of ardor in each new
        invagination of the strobed eclection, it

is near to being nothing as nothing is to
        this; as it rises, falling among shredded

lilacs, of a kind made kind with similarity,
        a Thomist knowledge tending plants in tidal

isolation; toward noon-time, standing, feeling
        the sun bleed warmth between folds of brown

fabric; there is a sprout needs pruning; a
        pitcher of cold water on a bench, so cold,

so piecemeal in the patchwork light; so
        separate with gold surrender circled in its

old elipses by a globed fatigue's reflection;
        it is near to being anything as anything to it.

Liturgical Chant

Hildegard of Bingen begins with a low
        hum's undercurrent, unbroken base for
        subsequent elaboration, and bends her

voice before the first breath finishes
        around the porcelain handle of a smooth,
        glass pitcher, pouring in a long stream

out of stars the present, now and now,
        to spatter softly in a basin, the solid current
        of her song submersing its own sound.

Dozing With Coffee

Only long enough to watch
a Polynesian girl from work
letting air out of someone's
tires, then I wake up spilling
coffee in my lap. It is

paneled with abstraction
this conglomerate of worlds,
and a warmth is soaking through
my clothes. I remember knowing,
in my dream, where a clock

was, in a laundromat.
When I looked, it was midnight,
or, more precisely, ten minutes
after, and there was an old
man reading in a green and

brown recliner. It seemed
a jumbled, pleasant city, but
that same night, driving fast,
we ran down members of a
color-guard. Their flags fell

wrinkled on the asphalt. A
cloud obscures the sun abruptly,
grey with moisture, ragged,
from its edges long, stark
shafts of sunlight spear. I am

outside in the garden, wist-
ful over autumn as the ducks
lift off the lake. The leaves
are falling drenched with hues,
a jade bug on a blossom.

Monsieur Transitif

Gamboling, gamboling,
all this morning spent
gamboling. First, in
the kitchen, pouring
coffee, I gamboled by
a cabinet. Then, sockless,
set off by the ceiling fan,
beside a thumb-tacked
map of Europe, I gamboled.

But now, bogged down
by grammar, I do not
gambol. Picking and
sorting for sense and pace,
the fireflies in my head
take seats, and around
my page the patient
world gets up, and goes
gamboling, gamboling.

Memorabilia

On April 12, 1976, Elvis drove
      his Jaguar through the gates of Graceland,
      smoking a cigar.

In the photo, taken by the collector,
      the cigar is clearly visible as the King
      looks left at oncoming traffic.

The collector has even drawn
      an arrow to it in Elvis' mouth
      with what appears to be some Wite-Out.

A moment later, Elvis turned right
      and proceeded to a Memphis
      shopping mall, where, stepping from his car,
      he casually let the cigar fall to the asphalt.

Elvis bought a cute little puppy at a pet store.

All of this is verified by a typewritten,
      signed letter from the collector, who
      followed Elvis that day.

Now here it is in a plexiglass case
      like enamel from the Buddha's tooth.
      Bidding starts at $175. For the cigar, of course.
      The dog is with Elvis.

ON ZHAO MENG-FU'S "WANG RIVER SCROLL"

—*Yuan Dynasty*

More interesting even
    than the mountain cottage

are the seven pine trees
    on a nearby slope. Alone,

except for scattered shrubs,
    they break the foggy distance

into fact, draw forth
    the gaze toward far peaks.

Name Dropping

I telephoned Allen Tate
    around 1986 or so
        to wish him a Happy Birthday.

He'd been dead a few
    years at that point
        but didn't seem a bit surprised.

I sensed, however,
    a hesitancy in his voice,
    uncertainty, perhaps, about
    why someone he'd never met
    was calling.

So I said "I'm a friend of
    Robert Penn Warren's."

He and I both realized then
    that, as things stood, one
        of us would have to be a moron.

Only after waking up
    and staggering off to pee
        did I think to check if it was really
        his birthday. And guess what?
        It was me.

The Death of Gérard de Nerval

    Hardly capable
of fastening a proper slipknot
in the frozen darkness, his fingers
        must have fought

    a clumsy moment
to close upon that writhing tail
the slender fangs held motion-
        less and pale.

    In his poetry,
one finds the near miss everywhere,
the spent recoil from the strike
        at the scaly air,

    but that morning,
dans la rue de la Vieille-Lanterne,
he bit the wick with such a flame
        it ceased to burn.

References

Pure conceptual geometry littered with religious
        relics, dunes, scorpions, atomic testing grounds,
        amplitude modulated aromatic somas where

my glasses are, and yet all previous landlords
        testify to my reliability; the sorts of relics found
        on any bedside table, but reified, afar, infused

by the prescriptions of the lenses, the amount
        of water left in the glass, where the moon is, for
        all previous landlords testify to my reliability.

Amplitudes the likes of which Ruy Lopez might
        have looped about the Renaissance, palpitations,
        pure conceptual geometries, atomistic, as light

moves from the glass of water to the lenses so
        all previous landlords testify to my reliability,
        caring only that my checks cleared, came in on

the first, when I left I cleaned the refrigerator,
        including the crisper, pulled the door to, having
        dusted the bedside table where my glasses were.

The Phoenix Riot, 1898

—Benjamin Mays's first memory in Greenwood County, SC, recounted in *Born to Rebel*

From such a fire,
        with the elective franchise,
        his father submissively bowing,
        his father at gunpoint saluting white men,
        all swirling upward in its smoke,

what species of bird could
        reasonably be expected to arise?

But the pine shadows, shaken
        over maimed confluences
        of muscle and tired memory, unspooled
        fresh senses from his soul.

Wounded voices became so quiet
        that winter, burnt cedar so cold,
        the bleak rattle of flames one evening
        broke upon more basic flame, brittle sheets
        of rebellion broke on a bedrock
        of rebellion.

Who can say exactly how it happened?

By spring, at any rate, the crack
        in the window pane, in the wren's
        egg, in the spine of his favorite book,
        in his heart, ran like wax from a single wick
        wherever he dared look.

SYDNEY LANIER PASSING
THROUGH ASHEVILLE, NC, 1881

White pants in an open carriage?
        A child's eye fixes on the like.

Having read no poems, what
        should you look for in a poet?

Their parents made them line up
        along a dirt lane to see him pass.

He was very ill. The white pants
        mostly, and the way he tried

to smile as the carriage lurched.
        He lost his concentration once,

then, smiling, said "they have no
        shoes on" to his wife, Mary,

reading next to him, who said not
        a word nor ever once looked up.

THE COELACANTH

*—believed until 1938 to have become extinct
60 million years ago*

Now *that* is a listless fish, deep-
        water dropout from the bothersome

surface, bulge-eyed, having plumbed
        every believable motive to reach

the lightless bottom. It works its
        primitive flippers just enough to keep

from plowing fully into silt, manages
        to hover a few feet above a total disavowal,

letting the currents move it laterally,
        conserving energy. Archaic beyond

dreaming, it predates the dawn of dinosaurs
        (a cumbersome fad of muscleheads

it wholly failed to notice), who battled
        for the choicer cuts while it gawked

in pitch darkness, barely even wanting
        to breathe its thimbleful of water.

How It Happened

A pebble

> kicked
> gardening
> clattered
> off a bamboo

>> shoot.

For another

> only
> the red
> flutter
> of a redbird

>> rising.

Dogen

> heard
> a goose
> honk
> and grew

>> feathers.

Southern Crescent

Turning westward where the kudzu
>climbs the various canopies of sweet gum
>and white oak and suddenly collapses like a great wave
>on the downward slope of pine trees and mimosas,
>we pass over a penny.

The elderly gentleman in front of me
>turns to look at the eight year old across the aisle,
>then he casts a glance at me, as if someone has spoken,
>as if he has overheard something, like the last half
>of a football score on someone's radio.

A long strand of Norfolk and Southern freight cars,
>rusty brown, with bright orange and green graffiti,
>flows past the window on the right-hand side,
>rolling with us, but slower, a strange visual effect, veering
>off slightly and descending.

Georgia versus Tulane? Auburn versus Florida?

I suspect a conference rivalry; an in-state
>contest involving all-white, segregated
>teams. Hands grasping hips in rain. No face masks.
>All the noses broken. Blood turning brown on orange
>jerseys, blackening the green.

He turns back finally, gazing out his window
>at the spirals of wisteria, moss on the stone pilings
>of the old bridge.

And it is as if the boy's voice never shouted,
>never rode on the shoulders of other shouts,
>as if he never leapt up, shouting, from the still-warm rails
>or juggled luck from hand to hand, no heat having faded
>from a year no longer legible.

Frog in Ivy

After a huge white strangely billowing
        tuft of cloud escapes the easternmost
        branches of the oak tree and withdraws

entirely beyond the porch to leave me
        staring into nothing but the stricken
        abstract curvature above my spouse's

car, a tree frog chirps in a pot of ivy
        next to me. Only once. And he seems
        to assume he has achieved his end:

that other frogs will suction their way
        down all surrounding trees and pioneer
        a set of small methodic paths through

grass and gravel like spokes of a sexual
        wheel collapsing inward to this ivy pot.
        Now, I cannot say there is no precedent

for this in Greek mythology, especially
        the wanderings of Dionysus, but come
        on, frog, who do you think you are?

CATULLUS IN THE AFTERLIFE

Once the purple cirrus orgies had subsided,
    I arranged myself among the arrogant harangues
    of starlight and began my corrective maneuvers,
    desiring moral insight over my empiric past,
    sterility of purpose over pleasant curiosity,
    depth of indecision over lenient proclivity.
    Carefully in fleecy tandem then eternity's concision
    circled in my hindsight and spun upward as if

singed by the recollection of lost love. My
    fingers clutched at the ache and were cut
    by antiquity's unkind concern, ragged ice among
    my eye's reluctant gel. Caesar lowered his cup
    to me, but I slapped it away. It was the last
    time I ever saw him. Cumulus formations covered
    us with urgent coils of rheumatoid contentment,
    dragging pallid hubris over ornery depression,

tranquilized amazement over turbulent ennui.
    My essence spun forth like a whisper wearing
    a spider web, like a blue spark turning on twin axles
    of pure light, past the privet roost of ordinates
    with cobweb wings upheld to slander false
    directions, past maidens in white dresses scaled
    with ramparts and bronze railings. Voices
    tickled out of voices like dust beaten out of

a carpet (quick-turning acronyms of endless
    interspersion, bristle-coned, world-barbed, from
    a song so luridly depictful as to spatter its own
    visage with a high-flung solstice flirt) until I was
    dispersed. Orchids fade and brighten in the scarlet
    folds that flutter along my breath these days. *Knees,
    knees, and blind aching*, I call. Whose cloud have
    I lost my way in, whose beautiful, stony clutter?

BY THE COMET'S LIGHT

Bark falls away from the tree.
The silver tea set tarnishes every
damned time you turn around
to the shade of a Darjeeling tea.

That perpetual, annoying yelp
you could not stop the idiot dog
tied up to the porch from always
yelping, stops without your help.

Cool breezes smear the borders
between breaths, cooler at each
cough. You ponder it instead
of giving drive-through orders.

Worse, in your dream tonight,
you stop outside a jewelry store
with a huge glass window, yet you
see no jewels. Only a blue, bright

hummingbird's reflection just
behind your head. It found you,
its humming seems to suggest, by
following a trail of ice and dust.

Formalities

One of us will soon
      be gone, tree,
      and I have not yet learned
      your proper name.

The woodpecker
      works you over
      every Spring, the worst
      of it on the side that faces
      west,

and my left knee
      bends a little less each Fall.

I'd like to be able
      to say more to you
      than "Poplar," after
      all these years, if only your
      Latin genus,

when I hoist myself,
      grumbling, our final
      afternoon together, to
      fling the last of my whiskey
      at the tulips.

Set Three: The Hedgehog's Dilemma

Arthur Schopenhauer, *Parerga und Paralipomena*: "A number of porcupines huddled together for warmth on a cold day in winter; but, as they began to prick one another with their quills, they were obliged to disperse."

DIALECTIC

Hate is simple.
        Love is complicated.

Hate like a fist
        lunges at its object.

Love is at rest,
        tangled in itself.

Love cannot remember
        why or why not.

Hate cannot
        resist its reasons.

Hate in its certainty
        is eager to explain itself.

Love, confused
        by its many complexions,

looks and looks
        and never learns enough.

TRYST IN THREE DIMENSIONS

One: Sunset

It is dusk among the genotypes
        and the flowerless invalids cascade
        across the aperture, braiding their

peevish archetypes together in one
        timid loop. Igneous trivia pulses in
        the marrow, mingling its crystalline

memory with meaty warmth, genetic
        predisposition. Oh, for the latinate
        sporedoms of the Cenozoic, the first

rare wave of angiosperms: the Rynia,
        ferny Medullosa. We lounged like chimps
        in the shade of the Lepidodendron,

closer than two petals, a string of
        pearls, strands of hair behind the ear,
        the crease of the clothing's orbit, a hinge

Two: Night

having opened and shut unobserved
        eleven times, aphids' feet navigating
        the pin, it opens, reveals all physical

space to be translucent diamonds, all
        physical space candescent for an instant,
        angularities ablaze with curvilinear

stitching, intestinal memory, two stones
        falling from the temple's cornice,
        arrested in all pivots, granular music

of our impact spun from the gut, closer
        than a hiccup or cough, coming to rest
        among orange, off-white flowers a while,

soil grasping our roughness with red
        ochre . . . less factual than plausible, less
        pantomime than popular geography

Three: Sunrise

we lay, plucked by a thornlessness
        in doubled vase, drifting negligently
        muted where a swan's neck circles

to itself within the water. This goes
        further than a physical bird's reflected
        wake and is concerned with categories,

being one as we like this in singleness
        to our composite natures seem: our
        several sub-variants of seed, of stalk,

in standing oceans, in deep sky deposits
        of white chalk. Purple, violet petals
        on the vine pervade the vivid intervals

between your lips and mine; pivotal voicings
        purr among rapacious morn; it is so cold . . .
        and look at what we have not worn!

Elle Fait Une Promenade

Interesting how it is when she walks forward,
        how her wake, with its memory of stillness,
            draws familiar deadlock through my thought's

inertia up into the branches of my eyes, how it
        rattles the brittle leaves; interesting too . . . how
            the colors deepen from the edges in, like curved

attention cupped within the retina, a ruptured
        pomegranate wrenching the iris . . . how, stopping,
            her shadow stirs the still, blue stream between us.

HER LAUGHTER

Made of the fifth
element, the flesh of angels.

Quintessence.

Not of earth, air,
fire, or water, in the least.

A conceptual plasma
such as dances in the air above
Alaska.

December to June

My decline, not yet pronounced,
       began this morning.

But you, dear, still have
       numerous career
       options open through
       the middle of next week.

Is it honorable of me, thus,
       to suggest a liaison
       between the two of us?

I have at last count
       only past accumulations
       of insanity and pregnant silence
       to persuade you with.

My breath moves
       beside your cheek
       like a cold stream past
       impossibly bright flowers.

THE VESUVIUS OF ORRERIES

Magma hardens around
    my mouth: 81 degrees longitude,
    32 degrees latitude.

Stars within moons within
    suns of sometimes cloudy
    quelque fois unclear perfumes
    of ancillary madness move
    among my teeth, damaged obstinacies
    arguing the issue at random angles,

(though I myself am still as flame).

Damnation but the pulse's brief,
    interminable tetanus of hallucination
    stings. I almost think at times that
    I could speak a word and have you
    hear it.

MEANDERING IN NEW ORLEANS

Below us, the Mississippi
    moves quietly, the water
    making only a low murmur
        as it runs along the levee.

Docklights flicker in the wake
    as the sun descends
    toward the Lac des Allemands.
        How much we two can take

depends. Therefore, you peel
    the rind from a mandarin
    orange. Your swift, thin
        fingers slow a bit to feel

the pressure of the sap
    below the skin, then draw
    the fruit apart in two raw
        wounds abruptly in your lap.

And as the sun goes down,
    you give me one to eat,
    the river making, at our feet,
        along the levee, a low sound.

He Catches Hell

A little longer,
a little longer
and the sharpest edges
will begin to blunt themselves.
A few more prepositions, a
few more verbs forgotten
and the argument may
finally turn in my favor;

her face, so angry,
may acquire the shadows
of interior turmoil, her words
the shape of her own pain
instead of my shortcomings.

A little longer,
a little longer
and her last goodbye
may seem, my god, some
other sort of word; the moon,
finally, supplanting the sun's
reason, may soften, almost,
her face into a tortured
resignation, and her eyes,
in the darkness, somehow
smile.

Still-life
After a Long Night

One fully expects
the table to give
way, let fruit
and fruit basket fall.

One expects
and is, therefore,
astonished when whole
stars remain aloft,

when the hesitant
blush of sunrise
flowers, and the birds,
long silent, sing.

THE STRESSED SYLLABLE

My second night in the apartment
        since before Christmas, this being March,
        I make a point of moving nothing, disturbing
        no dust. It all started when I stupidly said
        "yes" to my supervisor.

"Success," I always say, "means never saying no."

But when I told you about it
        you turned away from me,
        twisting the sheet across your hip,
        and whispered at the wall: "There's obsequious
        and then there is *obsequious*."

I lay there for three hours, watching
        a blade of light stab through the blinds
        with each passing car, estimating its outermost
        edges on the ceiling, thinking about the way
        you placed the emphasis on the second syllable
        of the second obsequious.

Then I threw the covers back
        and swung my feet down to the floor.

I believe you heard me, putting on
        my clothes, gathering my toiletries, maybe
        a little too loudly, but you lay there in your sheet.
        Goddamn, the streets of the Garden District
        are deserted at 4 A.M.

By Lake Pontchartrain

Inadequate meanders of preceding
        quaintness stir the heart and sullenly
        perform again all ancient failures,
        raising

and lowering the relevant national
        flags in alternating flourishes; red,
        yellow, red, white reticulations
        plumping

the fall breeze with harmless rage.
        I have no idea that my shoe is untied,
        but as I gaze toward the careless water
        I pull

up my sock. A sudden swell of
        querulous shadow quiets the sunlight
        for an instant, then its brightness
        crashes

along the rocky shore with added
        force. I try to trace the tangents drawn
        tight between all temporary meaning,
        suspend

the disparate world's debris
        a moment in the eye, to measure
        the collective exhalation of the
        tide, its

piecemeal ruin as it ravels
        over the rocks. If I find you again,
        I hope I will be adequately broken,
        amiss,

tangled up at last in the incidental
        tripe of things unspoken, to persuade
        you to come wading with my impure
        kiss.

Seven p.m. or So

Were this Louisiana,
>your headlights would be raking ivy
>on the fence-top right about now, blazing
>along yellow blossoms as far as the house allows,
>not quite to the rusted shed roof, blown away by Katrina,
>but close enough to draw my gaze there.

I would let my left foot slide
>from my right knee soon, draw my right foot up
>across my left knee, open my book again
>as if I were still reading something.

Were this Louisiana,
>I would contemplate the yellow blossoms,
>no less beautiful in darkness, knowing full well
>that the house is scented with baked salmon, basil,
>that the orange light on the rice cooker is still glowing
>in the far corner of the kitchen.

You'd come straight through the house
>to open the back door, your shadow flowing out
>through the grass to the ivy, rising up along the fence
>to the yellow blossoms, and my right foot would fall down
>from my knee as I closed my book and turned
>as if I were surprised to see you.

Parting, with a Sequel

Some lithic time upon a once
within a circle stream we walked.
Kind flakes of cold forgiveness blew about me
as you talked.

Not swift, not necessarily that slow,
the waters eddy backward as they flow.

But January's anger
foamed against the jagged bank, and jumbled
remnants of old letters washed about me
as you mumbled.

Too swift, however, to be safely swum,
the parts all being slower than the sum.

Bright suavity of broken
sunlight swirled among the sandalwood,
and you fell silent finally. You turned to see
if somehow I misunderstood.

Things recede or surge so much with us,
I said, *with all so simultaneous.*

But phrases spoken soon froze
solid. Words, like moss and water mingling,
became so twisted up they tightened with each
untangling.

Things are never only and thereafter
always and forever woe or laughter.

And so again we lay
some lithic waste of time upon the sand,
a ripple's length or less, rubbed smooth as rock,
where calm and rabid chaos ran.

Parking in Bayou Des Égarés

Mercury-amalgam ruminations
        reverse themselves mid-sentence,
        shattered into silver beads, endings, beginnings,
        scattered among intermediate meanings.

Across Acadiana's wreckage
        only the sexless light of stars,
        indifferent and centered, casts appropriate
        designs of shallow or deep shade, captures,
        across the jilted, Doric starknesses and lime-
        green sprays of foliage still spreading up the metopes,
        as we kiss, decay.

It is a cold night, chilly, even in a tunic
        and tri-corner hat, Elizabethan ruffles of frilled rust.

Constellations snag on lipstick stains,
        spilling out our raw thought's ripened
        orchestra of frets and strings.

And in this light (who knows
        how many millions of years old),
        your lips, your hands, appear peripheral
        to landscapes and livestock. Species follows upon
        species, fangs, talons, tumbling, until the advent
        of animal husbandry, specialized handicrafts,
        and this automobile with, of all things, fins.

Peasant Wedding Aftermath

—taking liberties with Breugel, 1567

Merely to feel her flesh, though its
Flanders vigor is worn away, though
keepsake tendons only of Walloon motifs
survive beneath a relic graft of gum and
pasty resin, is better than fresh beef.

As a mode of furnishing, at best,
his arm presents itself, a rink of lesser
grays engaged in a grotesque endeavor:
going out across the tablecloth, between
the empty pie tins, toward a severe

woman with a narrow face. She
seems an aggravating strength among
the weakened yawning of amassed pastels
and looks away from him on purpose
to peruse the scattered mussel shells.

His eyes, his countenance, remain
unseen. His hand, however, hesitates,
becomes a bit medieval in its artificial twist.
It ought to stop, retreat, but seems inclined
to falter past the meat toward her fist.

An Evening Out with Pharaoh

Six of the world's seven wonders
are gone, and rain emerges from the night
with aimless regularity. An owl hoots,
its eyes half closed against the light.

Water has penetrated to the heart
of things. Nothing is waterproof anymore.
It dampens the last dry sock at the bottom
back corner of every dresser drawer,

soaks through all paper towels
and beads on the inside of each flimsy,
cardboard core. Deep shadow floods out
into shallow darkness, fed up with me.

It pushes past, brushes my shoulder
like an angry son, sullen as a separate life.
Tonight I had dinner with a powerful man
who has made overtures to my wife.

His voice rolled under the table like
a cherry tomato, tapping the tip of my toe.
He reached with his fork, without asking,
and cut off a piece of my *petit gateau*.

A light-brown moth flutters down
from the filament, fatigued. Such things
take time, friend. Imagine how much longer
the pyramids may last against *my* wings.

Islamorada

Carved crystal dripping window light, red-
        orange light, yellow kitchen sunset light,
        your meaning wavers in the doorway, bright

with memory, expectation. You have asked
        me to open a jar, pointing to it on the counter,
        making a twisting motion, wasting no words.

Oh, I understand you well enough, but
        I stare awhile, remembering, who knows
        why, that waterfall beside the pool in the Keys,

backlit by night by colored lights. Your black hair
        wavered out through blackness as I buoyed your
        body up. I could twist a lid off easily then,

talking nonchalantly, gesturing. Nowadays
        I take in air and tense my gut. Maybe that's
        why I hesitate, recalling the garish light,

how it mimicked the water's movement on your
        legs as you climbed the ladder, how you motioned
        without speaking, offering a hand to help me.

Running Late in Yuyao

—Zhejiang Province, PRC

We stopped briefly before reaching
        the bridge, your eye distracted by some
        silk that might be suitable for a cheongsam.
        So I turned to the mountains with your purse
        in my left hand.

A brownish black goat planted
        a hoof in the dirt, lifted the other hoof,
        planted it, shifted, looking down a long
        draw toward an old woman washing pots
        in stream water.

Voices like water over the rocks,
        clashing, chaotic, unexpectedly quiet,
        carried up the hill, but you bought
        no silk. And I continued to hold your purse
        in my left hand.

The brownish black goat lowered
        its head to the stream, so fast and cold,
        so much louder suddenly than women
        or wind. I cannot remember if the bird sat
        in a nearby tree

or on one of the rocks to sing. But,
        as you looped your arm in mine and began
        walking down to cross the river, every voice
        inhaled, and in that hush I heard it: high notes
        in a clustered hurry.

Rhetorical Occasions

1.

Fermentation works its magic on our weather.
        Red leaves have become red wind, acidic wind,
        astringent, blown about the table like so much

lipstick on a napkin, radiating flawed remorse
        in spokes of briary shade and corked virtue. We
        both agree on this much. Blonde and jet-black

weaves of anger and self-doubt shake dandruff
        on our pastries, spilling nostalgia from the saucer's
        edge. And, again, you commence your authentic

Norse chanting: an aspirate followed by a sibilant
        followed by an alveolar. There is precious little
        archaeological evidence that this was ever done.

Or why. Or why a modern advocate should under-
        take it now. To make the clouds move lower?
        To separate the noise of the rain from the wetness

of thunder? Not that ignorance can slow you.
        But much to my amazement, a light smattering
        of letters begins to tap at the awning. Before long,

type-writer keys are descending, slanted, upside
        down, alongside raindrops that are always angled
        rightly. The ruddy braid of your singing spoils

everyone's appetite, though no-one has the nerve
        to say it. I push my plate away. You open your
        mouth even wider. Am I supposed to rush madly

into your arms now? Move closer like the clouds?
        Shed my armor like a sous chef? Like a besieger
        of Jerusalem? Is that your immature expectation?

2.

Clean patience earlier, but now the providential
        hum of broken hours in the brain is pulsing,
        high-pitched like piano wires, glass chips pecking

at pavement, patterned intonations interwoven
        with broad heresies of rhythmic bass, and I sense
        my ruin. The age of progress ends with a steamy

hiss. If only you would look up from your book,
        our lives might be so different. You have read
        to the bottom of a page and now grasp the corner

of the next one, gazing back as if to gather insight
        from the pattern of preceding punctuation. Perhaps
        I can offer some assistance here, stranded though

I am on a separate mountaintop. I initiate a series
        of rapid shifts from chest to falsetto registries in
        order to yodel some basic literary pointers across

the coffee table. But snow devils whirl my truth
        toward the kitchen, dropping it in powder drifts
        against the refrigerator. Flurries and snowsqualls

cover the footprints that might have led me safely
        to the vicinity of your slippers. From there I might
        have felt about for the edge of the sofa cushion.

Accumulations of ice snap the guide rope I hung
        between the side-table lamp and the front door.
        Look up! I am clinging to the edge of a crevasse!

My fingertips are becoming very uncomfortable!
        Yo del ay ee oo. Just turn the page, why don't you?
        Get on with it. Because even from here, through

my educational transparencies of 1750s European
        Imperial rivalry to control the Ohio River Valley,
        through concentric electromagnetic fields that spin

my compass needle, I see the silhouettes of two
        figures running through fierce rain to one another
        despite the howling prospect of financial doom.

A Note on Surplus Value

You had plucked the last grape or else
harvested a succulent fruit of some kind
that would not ripen again in your lifetime,
when you paused without knowing why

and remembered your first love.
She smiled at you again as if you had
forgotten she was there, extended a blue
pomegranate, a magnolia blossom perhaps,

held it out to you in a way that suggested
a generous heart. But you wondered
what it was. You thought mostly about
figuring it out. And she could not tell you.

So she lowered the bouquet again, put
down the pomegranate, pear, persimmon,
or small berry. And as you looked out
finally at the withering fields, where nothing

similar to what you now held in your
hand would ever grow again in your life,
you lost your appetite at last. You opened
your fingers a little, offered it to your wife.

Ozymandias at Odds

Out in the garden, reading Shelley's lies
        about a dome of colored glass, an elbow
                reaches through my own reflection

from the kitchen window, testing the ties
        on the orchid spikes, then watering the aloe.
                Farther in, past a glittering confusion

of eyeglass lenses, I look for your eyes,
        concentrating, as they must be, on the slow
                debris of sunlight circling the onion.

Last Meeting

When they no longer knew each other's names,
they laid their flowers beside their favorite
pairs of shoes and extended their best memories
out across the water. His involved the games

their son played, the carpet he liked to crawl
around on, her face made beautiful by worry
as the baby stood the first time. They traveled
eastward, while hers, with their sizzle and sprawl

of pancake batter complaining on the stove,
went west. And where they finally met again,
somewhere far away from land, drawn out almost
to nothingness, a school of delicate sunfish dove.

www.ingramcontent.com/pod-product-compliance
Lightning Source LLC
Chambersburg PA
CBHW020340170426
43200CB00006B/444